IMAGES
of America

REMEMBERING DETROIT'S

OLYMPIA STADIUM

IMAGES
of America

REMEMBERING DETROIT'S
OLYMPIA STADIUM

Robert Wimmer

ARCADIA

Published by Arcadia Publishing,
an imprint of Tempus Publishing, Inc.
3047 N. Lincoln Ave., Suite 410
Chicago, IL 60657

Printed in Great Britain.

Library of Congress Catalog Card Number: Applied For.

For all general information contact Arcadia Publishing at:
Telephone 843-853-2070
Fax 843-853-0044
E-Mail sales@arcadiapublishing.com

For customer service and orders:
Toll-Free 1-888-313-2665

Visit us on the internet at http://www.arcadiapublishing.com

For Diane—
Who smiled through it all,
changing seats at the Old Red Barn

CONTENTS

ACKNOWLEDGMENTS

Grateful acknowledgment is made to the following individuals that contributed photographs and information to this book: Lydia Ernatt, Bruce Lathi, Art Whalen, Jake Austin, Ken Lindsay, Terry Rickman, Greg Innis, Bill Clements, Dennis Rybant, Marcia Kamin, Larry Kosebia, Bright Imaging Company, Jim Reed, Ed Fabiano, Dwayne Labakas, Lincoln Cavalieri, John Morrison and the Hockey Information Service, Ted Lindsay, Jimmy Skinner, Don Albertson, Lynn Kopiczko, the family of William and Bernie Opalewski, Bud Howland, and for those I missed, *mea culpa.*

INTRODUCTION

When *Detroit's Olympia Stadium* came out in December of 2000, I thought it was over. I had told the story of the building and an era in Detroit that was a second home to many people of all walks of life, from the fans, the employees, the entertainers, and the players. Such was not to be. Within a couple months, I had received calls and letters from all over the U.S. and Canada. For the most part their statements were, "It's a very good book. I read it over several times and shed a few tears. Olympia was like a second home and family to me, but why didn't you mentioned the popcorn lady, the other great shows like KISS, Emerson, Lake and Palmer, Paul McCartney and Wings, Dorothy Hamill and Peggy Fleming, the ushers, the other juniors and recreation teams that skated there"—and the list went on. Many of the former employees who called or wrote said they had photos of themselves and coworkers they wanted to share and so I called my publisher and told him about the calls and letters. Thus, *Remembering Detroit's Olympia Stadium* was born.

Thanks to modern technology and the Internet, I was able to find some of the employees, such as the ushers and game-night officials. Through a couple concession workers (who in 2001 were now with the Red Wings at the Joe Louis Arena, after having worked at the Olympia over 20 years ago) we started to find people and photographs.

When I called some of the former employees, who were scattered all over the country, they were curious at being remembered. Then the excitement started in their voices and it was like we were back in the '60s and '70s at the "Old Red Barn." One of the ushers who used to let us sit in empty seats in his section is now 84 years old and living only 10 minutes from me. I hadn't seen him since they closed the building in 1980. Another is living in Dearborn in an assisted living center, and another has an apartment in a senior citizens complex. It's like they all started to come out of the woodwork. Some are still working the press box at the Joe today.

I myself had been around the Olympia since the '50s. Actually, I played the Olympia in the '40s appearing with hundreds of others in the Grinnells piano concerts. But my real start came in the late '50s when I was a beginning freelance photographer. Having no press affiliations I would buy a standing room ticket and then proceed to the visiting teams bench area. There were four rows of seats behind the bench with no glass or screen. The coach walked behind the bench in front of the fans. Often, if a player needed a stick at the end of the bench, the trainer would hand it to a fan behind the bench and they would pass it down to the players. Fans could reach out and touch the players—they were that close. However, by the third period, with the players sweating, it could tax your sense of smell and sometimes their language was of the locker room variety.

At one game as I was trying to get some photos, Mrs. Adams, who had a box behind the visitors' bench asked me who I was. I told her I was trying to learn the trade and just had a standing room ticket. She asked me if I would take a couple photos of her guest in her box. I said no problem. When the game started I headed upstairs to sit on the stairs and watch the game. Photographers with passes were allowed to sit on the lower stairs to take pictures, the fans on the upper stairs. Occasionally the fire marshall would show up and the ushers would clear the stairs. Minutes later, the fans returned to the stairs again. The following game I showed up with several copies of Mrs. Adams' group and gave them to her. She asked me for a bill and I said forget it. She never said anything about me taking photos without a pass, so it was worth it. The next game she called me over and asked me for my business card, which I didn't have so I wrote down my name, address, and phone number on a piece of paper and gave it to her.

About a week later I received a letter from Nick Londes, who was the general manager of the Olympia Stadium, along with a building pass for all events courtesy of Mrs. Adams. Thanks to this lady's generosity, I began a love affair with the Olympia that was to last over 20 years until the building closed in 1980. Farewell my lovely, we still miss you.

One
THE PEOPLE
BEHIND THE SCENE

Opposite the Grand River end was the Olympia Organ, located in sections 30 and 31. This photo from the '40s shows organist Merle Clark playing. The organ was used at Red Wing games and also for public skating after the Monday night amateur games.

Before the Zamboni first appeared at the Olympia in May of 1957 (a model FL-69), a crew had to clean the ice by hand, pulling a barrel filled with warm water to melt the top layer of ice into a smooth surface.

Getting popcorn ready for the hockey fans, on New Years Eve 1962, are Dorothy Wellman and Lydia Ernatt. The Rangers and Wings played to a 1-1 tie that night.

Ushers Ed Fabiano and Frank Mitchalek usually worked sections 14 and 16 in the arena under the press box. They are wearing the blazer type ushers coats, which replaced the old military style.

NHL Off-Ice Officials Pete Daniels (left) and Bill Clements take a few minutes to talk to fans between periods. Clements, who was director of off-ice officials for the NHL at Olympia, was a former linesman in the National Hockey League.

These are Olympia Stadium maintenance workers, from left to right: Jim Hook, unidentified, Red Wings Assistant GM Jim Skinner, and Frenchy Fuquay—at work on the ice in December of 1968. Frenchy was the Zamboni driver during the Wings games in the '60s and '70s.

NHL Off-Ice Officials' Supervisor Bill Clements takes time to confer with Bob Watson in the penalty box at the Wings' March 14, 1973 game against Montreal. In the early days, there was only one penalty box and an usher sat between the players. Later, two boxes were installed and the off-ice officials sat between the two benches.

Lydia Ernatt sells Ice Follies balloons to the fans.

The NHL Olympia off-ice officials visited the Wings training camp at Port Huron for press day. They are, from left to right: (front row) Ken Hankala, Chuck Sneddon, Fred Pike, and Dave Bryant; (standing, back row) unidentified, Bob Blow, Gerry Waechter, Bob Kennear, and Jesse Thomas.

Usher Bernie Opalewski discusses some building problems with Olympia building superintendent Jake Austin.

April 1, 1969, Lydia Ernatt presents a large 40th birthday card to Gordie Howe. Lydia had the card at her station and had fans and employees sign it. They are, from left to right: Howe, Michigan Hall of Famer Ron Kramer, Red Wing Alumni President Joe Carveth, and Free Press Sportswriter Jack Berry. Howe's birthday was March 31.

Former Beatle Paul McCartney, then touring with Wings, took time out to pose with concession worker Lynn Kopiczko backstage.

A banner hangs from the balcony for Wings great Gordie Howe. Many people preferred to sit in the first couple rows in the balcony rather then downstairs, claiming it was the best seat in the house even though they had to walk up 101 steps to get there. An escalator was installed in 1974 with the new addition. The box below was one of four installed, in each corner of the building. These were the first private boxes installed in an indoor arena. Lincoln Cavalieri, then Vice President of the Wings, started the idea and they were sold out immediately. Eventually more boxes were added throughout the Olympia. Today, most arenas around the world have followed Cavalieri's innovation. The boxes are a main source of income for teams and arenas.

The girls were on the job making popcorn in November 1968, from left to right: Lydia Ernatt, Wanda (waving), and Lee Denacor in front.

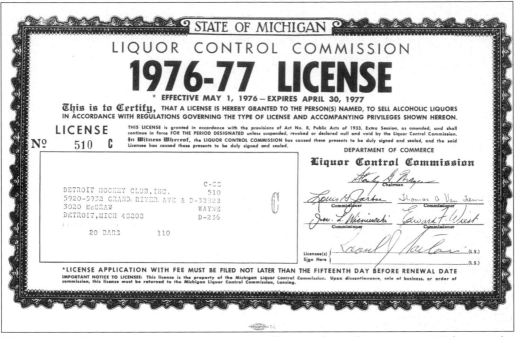

This is the 1976-77 Liquor License, giving the Olympia the right to operate 20 bars in the building.

Dr. John Finley, the Red Wings Team Physician, takes time to talk over the old days with Mrs. Helen Adams, the wife of the former Wings Coach and General Manager, outside the Wings bench corridor.

Usher Goodie Hook keeps an eye on the young fans as the Beatles perform at the August 13, 1966, 2:30 p.m. concert at the Olympia. Unlike the first concerts in 1964, the '66 concerts did not sell out.

Concession workers Wanda and Lydia posed with the Detroit Police detail at a Wings game. The Police detail, from left to right, are: Dick Chovich, unidentified, Ray Yates, Orval Salsbury, Carl Dolechek, and Bill Riggs.

Backstage at an ice show, the ice crew poses for a picture. Note the old style white sweaters.

Getting ready to celebrate a New Years event at the front counter facing Grand River are, from left to right: Jackie, Lynn Kopiczko, unknown, Elsie Dargan, Lydia Arnatt, and Ellen Maisel.

Up in the Olympia Room during a Red Wing press conference are front office staff and coaches, from left to right: Chris Jacobs, Wings Coach Bobby Kromm, Assistant Coach Billy Dea, unknown, and Marvin Mews.

Ushers at the ice show, posing during a break in the action are, from left to right: Jack Walton, Ed Fabiano, Frank Mitchalek, and Jerry Opalewski.

Concession Manager Roule Satori talks to Elsie Dargan and Lydia Ernatt. When Lydia started in 1957 she was getting paid $5.00 for the walk-ins before the game and intermission. They did not do clean up then.

William Opalewski and son Jerry fill the water tank between periods at a Wings game. The barrel-like wagon had two white-wall car tires and was pulled around the ice after shoveling off the loose snow to put down a smooth sheet of ice.

Justine Muske, who with her husband Dr. Florian Muske took care of the Red Wings dental needs, is given a gift set of bracelets by Detroit's finest, from left to right: Jerry Majeski, Sgt. Al Barlitto, and Carl Dolechek in the hall outside of the Wings dressing room. The people who worked at the Olympia were very close-knit group, almost like a second family.

Lydia Arnatt, known as "the Popcorn Lady," gets ready for the doors to open so that she can sell hot buttered popcorn. The photo in the back shows Gordie Howe scoring on a penalty shot at a New Years Eve game against Toronto's Johnny Bower.

Two
THE MEDIA AND
THE PRESS

Detroit News Hockey Beat Writer Vartan Kupelian, Dennis Tanner, Rick Shook of the AP, Chuck Klonke of the AP, and Jerry Green, of the *Detroit News*, enjoy a free pre-game meal in the press box lounge located in the balcony.

Radio announcer Vince Doyle, *Hockey Night in Canada's* Dick Beddows, and Public Relations Director Al Coates take a few minutes to discuss the game. Beddows was famous for wearing his dressy hats on the air, and was the fancy dresser on Channel 9's telecast on Saturday's *Hockey Night in Canada* long before Don Cherry came on the scene.

Channel 4's Jim Forney interviews Goalie Jim Rutherford. Rutherford went on to become the General Manager of the Hartford Whalers, which later became the Carolina Hurricanes.

Members of the Detroit media get ready to play a charity exhibition game as they welcome their superstar Goalie-Weatherman Sonny Eliot with the traditional crossed sticks salute.

Red Wings Public Relations Director Ron Cantera interviews Wings Statistician Morris Moorawnick during training camp media day in Port Huron.

Wings Statistician Morris Moorawnick gives his opinion of the food in the pressroom, while reporters Vartan Kupelian of the *Detroit News*, and Dennis Tanner and Rick Shook of the AP watch Morrie chow down.

Mark Doc Andrews, Barry Smades of the *Oakland Press*, and Press Box Manager Hugo Costillo enjoy a pregame chat.

Public Relations Director Elliott Trumbull relaxes in his newly revamped second-floor office at Olympia as he gets ready for the 1959-60 NHL season. Behind Trumbull is a chart listing all the players owned by the Wings, where they are playing, and their up-to-date records.

This is the first Red Wings guide and fact book published by Elliott Trumbull's office in 1960. It sold for 50¢ at the concession stands.

Who's interviewing who? Goaltender Roger Crozier takes over the mike to interview Wings Announcer Bruce Martyn at the Wings training camp in Port Huron on Media Day.

Channel 9's Don Daly of Windsor interviews General Manager Alex Delvecchio up in the Olympia Room.

Red Wing announcers Sid Abel (seated) and Bruce Martyn (standing) interview NHL Referee Frank Udvari between periods in their booth high in the balcony. Abel held almost every position in the Wings organization from player, coach, general manager, and goodwill ambassador to radio and TV color man over his Hall of Fame career.

This item began to appear in homes around Detroit during the 1964-65 season as the Wings took their TV games to UHS on all-sports channel 50, WKBD. Since most TVs at that time didn't have the UHS channels, people brought this converter and hooked it on their receivers. From 1964-65 on, all televisions that were made had to have both VHS and UHS channels. Another popular TV show on TV 50 then was the controversial *Lou Gordon Show*.

Public Relations Director Elliott Trumbull watches TV weatherman Sonny Eliot put on his beard and makeup to play Santa Claus for the Wings 1964 Christmas Party. This office was on the first floor with the players chart again in the background. Trumbull was the one who started the Red Wings' players and family Christmas Party as well as many public relations innovations that are in standard use today.

This is the corner of Grand River and Hooker in the early '60s, with the Detroit Pistons office next to the drug store. The Pistons played at the Olympia before moving downtown to Cobo Hall. Note that cars parking on Grand River were legal then, during the day.

In the downstairs press box in section 14 and 16 on the McGraw side, teletype operators and reporters watch the action down below on the ice. Later, the press box moved up into the balcony when the building was expanded in 1974-75.

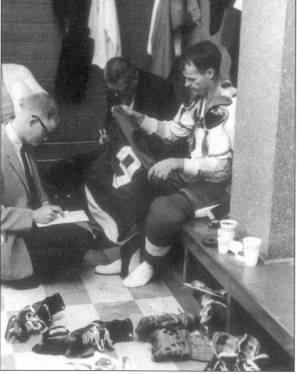

Super Fan Ron Cameron interviews Wings Defenseman Terry Harper. Harper was a defenseman for 19 seasons in the NHL with Montreal, Detroit, LA, St. Louis, and Colorado—before retiring in 1981. Cameron had several sports shows around the Detroit area in the 1970s.

After the game, reporters had to move in close to get interviews in the Wings dressing room. Most dressing rooms were quite small, with poor ventilation. After a few minutes, everybody was sweating as the room became hot and steamy. Some of the NHL dressing rooms had rats and poor plumbing. The worst arena in the Original 6 era was the Boston Gardens. In Chicago, the players had to walk down a flight of steps to get to their dressing room in the basement.

Enjoying a pregame meal is Red Wings Forward Dennis Polonich, who was sitting out this game. On the right is writer Tom Henderson. The writer in the middle is unknown.

Don Daly on TV 9 in Windsor interviews former player, scout, and coach Billy Dea. Dea served as coach in the 1981-82 season.

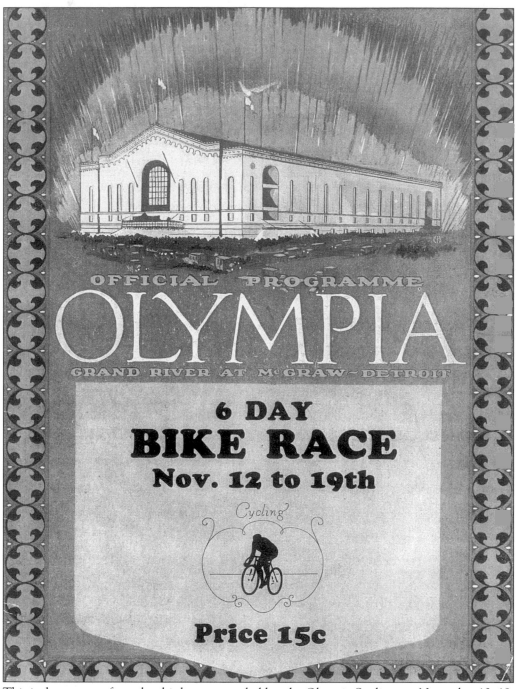

OFFICIAL PROGRAMME

OLYMPIA

GRAND RIVER AT McGRAW - DETROIT

6 DAY
BIKE RACE
Nov. 12 to 19th

Cycling

Price 15c

This is the program from the third event ever held at the Olympia Stadium on November 13–19, 1927. It was the First International Six-Day Bicycle Race. At that time J.L. Woods was the Chairman of the Board and General Manager. John C. Townsend was the Vice President and Otto Kern of Ernst Kern Co. was on the board. There were also stories and advertisements for the Detroit Cougars hockey team season coming up. The program also had a story on the new house manager, Percy Lesueur, who was manager of Windsor Border Cities Arena (now Windsor Arena). Lesueur was also a star goalie for Ottawa. He was inducted into the NHL Hall of Fame in 1961 as a player.

34

Three
THE OLD TIMERS
AND THE ALUMNI

These two old timers were a part of the Wings from the '30s up to the final days of the building. Normie Smith (left) played on the first two Stanley Cups Detroit won in 1936 and 1937. He was also the winning goalie in the longest playoff game ever played. The game was played on March 24 and 25, 1936, against the Montreal Maroons. The game went into six overtime periods before Mud Bruneteau scored 116:30 in the overtime. Detroit won 1-0. Lefty Wilson was the Wings trainer on three Stanley Cups and as a trainer in those days he was also the spare goalie. Three times he had to suit up during a game to replace an injured goalie. He replaced Terry Sawchuk on October 10, 1953, and shut out the visiting Canadiens the rest of the game. He also played for Toronto and Boston.

Five of the alumni, who played during the 1930s, checkout Red Doran's New York Americans jacket in the Alumni Room. They are, from left to right: Normie Smith, Ebbie Goodfellow, Doran, Rollie Roulston, and Doug Young.

Getting ready to hawk tickets for an upcoming "Old Timers Versus the Current Red Wings" charity game, from left to right, are members Ebbie Goodfellow, Tommy Smith, Lou Cromwell, Normie Smith, and Stu Evans.

Checking out the goalie stick used by Lorne Chabot of Montreal, in the longest game played in 1936, are members Joe Carveth, Rollie Roulston, Carl Liscombe, Ebbie Goodfellow, Red Doran, Sid Abel, Stu Evans, John Sherf, Normie Smith, and Don Grosso.

Alumni members take time to pose at a get together. They are, from left to right: Joe Carveth, Carl Mattson, Alex Delvecchio, Red Kelly, Art Bogue, Bill Gadsby, and Budd Lynch.

The Alumni team had their photo taken prior to their February 27, 1976 Old Timers game. They are, from left to right: (front row) Johnny Rea, Marty Pavelich, Nic Cinor, Jimmy Peters, Bob Brown, Tom Shaw, Bill Gadsby, and Billy Dea; (standing) Dr. C. Boone, Danny Olesevich,

Joe Klukay, Marc Reaume, Doug Barkley, Jerry Abel, Alex Delvecchio, Glen Skov, Joe Carveth, Leo Reise, Hal Jackson, Jack Stewart, Jimmy Orlando, Rollie Roulston, Jack Roberts, Mike Kandt, and Ted Lindsay.

Remembering the old days while relaxing in the referees dressing room after an Old Timers game are Budd Lynch, Harry Lumley, Rollie Roulston, and Sid Abel.

Ready to do battle again, the Old Timers get set to take the ice. They are, from left to right: Red Doran, Jack Stewart, Hal Jackson, Joe Carveth, Carl Liscombe, and Ted Lindsay. This photo was taken in the visiting teams dressing room.

Enjoying a little relaxation after a Monday night meeting in the Alumni Room, are, from left to right: (seated) Nic Cinor, Lefty Wilson, Nick Libbett, Johnny Wilson, Carl Liscombe, and Jerry Abel; (standing) Bobby Kromm, Joe Klukay, Bill Gadsby, and Dennis Hextall.

Between periods with the coach, are, from left to right: Marty Pavelich, Red Kelly, Coach Tommy Ivan, and Bill Gadsby. In this photograph, they enjoy a few minutes of remembering the good old days.

Practice time brings out many of the players getting ready for the next charity game, from left to right: (kneeling) Lions' star Darris McCord, Nic Cinor, Lions' Ron Kramer, and Roger Pineau; (standing) Joe Saunders, Red Doran, photographer J.D. Charlie McCarthy, the author, Lions' Quarterback Earl Morrow, and Joe Klukay.

The family and guest alumni party usually included a skate and refreshments up in the Alumni Room. Tony Wisne and Red Doran (back) bring the kids up for treats after skating.

After a practice skate, the alumni retire to their room up in the back of section 27 for refreshments. Some of the alumni include, from left to right: (seated) Joe Carveth and his wife Rita; (standing) Art Bogue, Red Raney, Mike Kandt, Tony Wisne, and Larry Wisne.

The alumni team and the Pico team take time out from a scrimmage to pose for a team photo. The alumni played a lot of exhibition and practice games with local teams.

Is this fun or fund raising after a meeting? The guys are seen here enjoying some fellowship and gamesmanship. They are, from left to right: (seated) Joe Klukay, Red Raney, Bobby Kromm, Art Bogue, Bill Gadsby, and Eddie Sophiea; (standing) unknown, Lefty Reed of the Hockey Hall of Fame, and Eddie Giacomin.

The referee, Budd Lynch, prepares to call another Old Timer's. Budd has been around the Wings since after World War II. He has been one of the finest goodwill ambassadors for the Wings and hockey for over a half century. Into the 21st century he was still announcing at Wings games at the Joe Louis Arena.

Four
THE SHOWS AND
THE ENTERTAINERS

This is one of the many ice show extravaganzas that appeared at the Olympia over the 50 years it was in operation. Shows such as *Holiday on Ice*, the *Ice Follies*, the *Ice Capades*, the *Hollywood Ice Review* all played here in Detroit. Below are samples of the tickets and the prices to buy them.

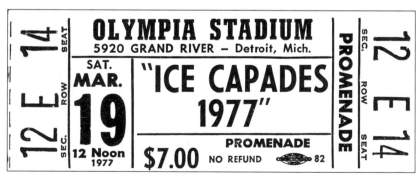

Costumes and choreography were always one of the major attractions in different numbers at ice shows. From the front, the headpieces look large and heavy, but from the rear the viewer can see they were light and very thin.

This is a copy of the cover of the 1938 *Ice Follies* program. In early days, the name of the arena was used on the cover, but later, for economic reasons a generic cover was used. Thus, for the whole season all the programs were the same in every city.

OLYMPIA

Presents

ICE FOLLIES OF 1938

UVENIR PROGRAM — TWENTY-FIVE CENT

Dorothy Hamill, of the *Ice Capades*, performs one of several numbers she was featured in. She was one of many of the top skaters in the world who appeared in Detroit, such as Sonja Henie, Richard Button, Peggy Fleming, and Barbara Ann Scott. At left is usher Mike Basala, who was assigned to guard the ice show stars and their dressing rooms, during all their performances.

The circuses were always big crowd pleasers in Detroit. The animals and wagons were kept in the back parking lot. But as more then one employee has always said, the circus was here for a week, the smell stayed around for a month. Back in the 1940s, the Barnes Bros. Olympia Circus also featured the Lone Ranger and Silver as one of their acts. The Lone Ranger originated in Detroit on radio and was one of the most popular fictional characters in the country.

The Detroit Red Wings played the Washington Capitals at 4 p.m. on January 22, 1978, beating them 6-3. After the game, KISS—the hottest rock group in the country at that time— performed a two-night stand to sellout crowds.

The wild costumes and loud music drew rock fans to KISS all over the world. Their boots and make-up had promoters lined up begging for a date in their city and arena. Below, KISS has their special stage scenery and equipment, with flashing lights driving the crowds to a fever pitch.

Ring Attendants Jerry and Norbert Opalewski help Baron Von Raschke regain his fighting composure in a wrestling match at the Olympia. Wrestling has always been a top draw in Detroit.

Lou Martinez, left, and Dick the Bruiser, along with Ring Attendant Norbert Opalewski, head out to do battle. The wrestlers seem to be friends here, but in the ring? Tell me this wasn't real. One of Dick the Bruiser's biggest matches was on April 27, 1963, when he took on suspended Lions football star Alex Karras after a much ballyhooed bar fight at the Lindell Bar in downtown Detroit.

The boys all get together for a group picture before heading out to perform in the ring. The group, from left to right, consists of: Jimmy Valient, Norbert Opalewski, Manager Bobby "the Brain" Heenan, Johnny Valient, and Jerry Opalewski.

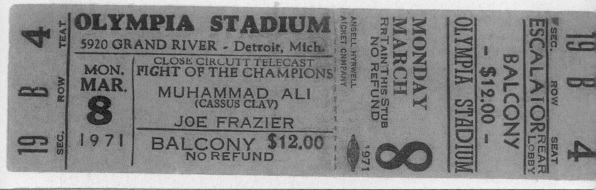

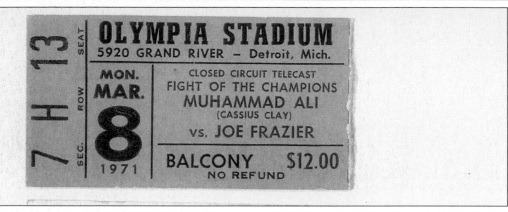

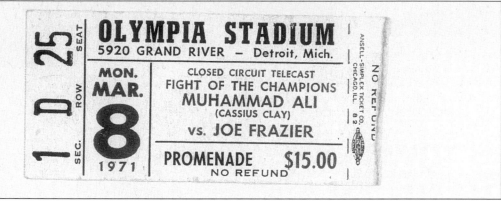

Here are three tickets and stubs. They were for the March 8, 1971 closed-circuit telecast fight between Muhammad Ali (Cassius Clay) and Joe Frazier. However, the ticket at the top was counterfeit. See if you can spot four differences between it and the bottom two. Boxing fans were buying these bogus tickets for $60 a pair. But Detroit Patrolman Jerry Morton of the Central Morality Squad discovered the tickets were fakes when he noticed four mistakes on them. The misspellings included Cassius Clav, circuit spelled circutt, company spelled cnmpany, and seat spelled teat. The counterfeiter pleaded guilty to a charge of scalping tickets and was sentenced to 60 days in jail by visiting Recorder's Judge William J. Sutherland of Taylor. Police said the scalper was selling the tickets for $50 each before he made the deal with Morton for two for $60.

54

One of the annual programs at Olympia was the Michigan Annual Music Festival, held this year on June 4, 1950. Grinnell's Music Stores sponsored the show. The piano players were all student of local teachers who gave lessons in their homes after school. Grinnell's at one time was the largest chain of music stores in the Detroit area.

OLYMPIA REVIEW
SPORTS MAGAZINE

"Battle of Champions"

Detroit DIAMOND BELT Champs

VERSUS

Detroit GOLDEN GLOVES Champs

MAY 9, 1941

Bernard J. Opalewski

PROCEEDS FOR WAR RELIEF IN BRITAIN   U.S. Department of State Reg. No. 348

Price 15c

This is a fight program from May 9, 1941, for the Golden Gloves and Detroit Diamond Belt Champs. Proceeds were used for war relief in Britain. It would be seven more months before the U.S. would enter the war, after the attack on Pearl Harbor on December 7, 1941.

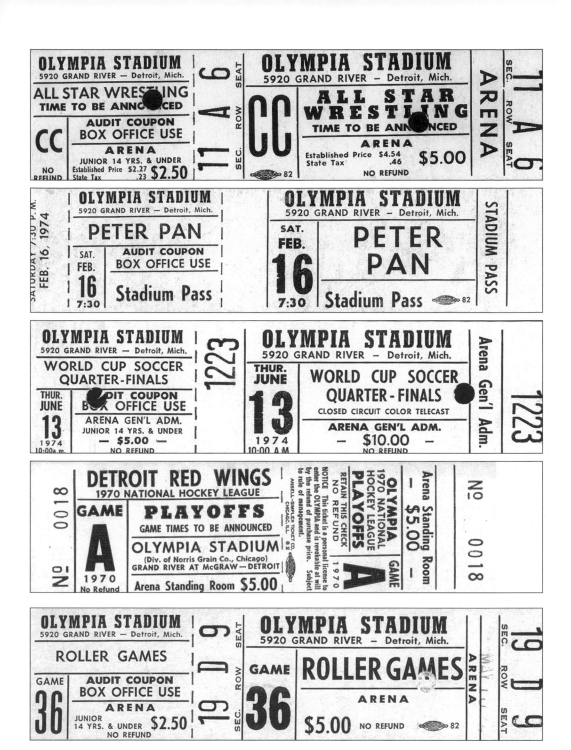

How many of these events did you attend? Did you get to see Isaac Hayes in concert?

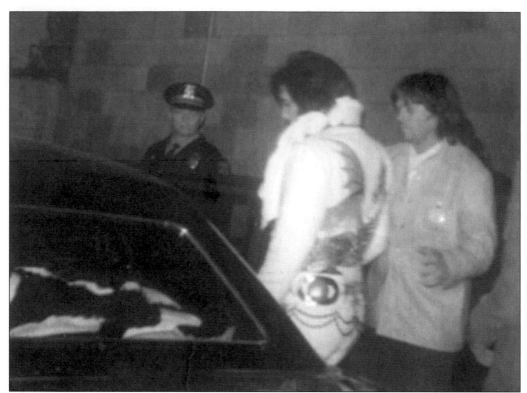

Elvis is seen leaving Olympia after a concert. Photographers were not allowed to take photos during the King's concert, but one employee managed to snap off a photo as he was leaving. Below is a pair of unused tickets for the April 22, 1977 concert at the Olympia Stadium. Showtime was 8:30 p.m. and cost only $12.50. Can you imagine what a pair would cost today if Elvis were still alive?

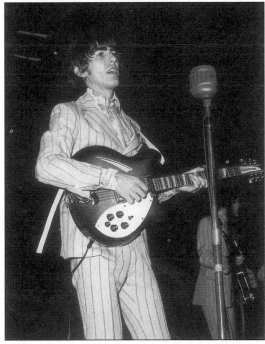

The girls screamed and went wild as the four lads from Liverpool, England, took over the music world in the '60s. The Beatles made two trips to Detroit, one in 1964 and another in 1966. Arena seats for the August 13, 1966 concert sold for $5.50. The two concerts performed in 1966 failed to sell out, but the Olympia showed a profit of $25,585.98 for the two performances. The photo on the right features George Harrison.

Police and ushers moved into the crowd of young girls during the concert to keep them from rushing the stage. A couple days later, in Cleveland, a mob estimated at 3,000 stormed the stage. The noise was so bad that policemen were seen putting bullets in their ears to keep out the noise. For some reason, almost all teenagers occupied the front seats with very few adults nearby.

Seen here on the left, John Lennon smiles and gives the girls his best shot. In his later years John would become an artist and gain fame in other areas before he was shot in front of his apartment hotel. On Sunday September 6, 1964, the Beatles did two shows. The Ronettes, consisting of Elaine Spector, Estelle Bennett, and Nedra Talley, were the opening acts for the Beatles, as were Barry and Vern of the Remains.

George Harrison and drummer Ringo Starr perform while some fans watch from the balcony behind the stage. Note the Montreal (Canadiens) and Red Wings scoreboard on the balcony. Paul McCartney was the most sought after of the Beatles, for his looks. After the Beatles broke up, he toured with his own group, called Wings. The two 1966 concerts took in over $100,000 for the two 30-minute performances. After the 7 p.m. concert, the group escaped on a chartered Greyhound bus to Cleveland, while their limos were used as a decoy to distract fans.

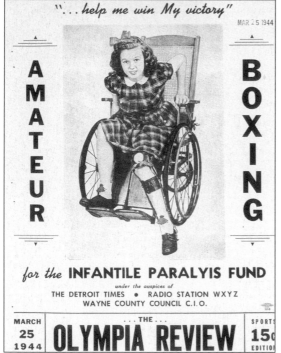

Tommy "Hit Man" Hearns gets ready to square off in a charity match against Bob Beruregard, a J.W. Thompson ad executive. Handling the announcing and refereeing duties is Michigan State Boxing Commissioner and former boxing champion Chuck Davey.

This is the cover of a March 25, 1944 amateur boxing program for the Infantile Paralyis Fund. The program was sponsored by the *Detroit Times* newspaper, which folded in the early 1960s and was taken over by the *Detroit News*.

Indoor Box Lacrosse, called such because it was played on the hockey floor with all the board and backstops in place, tried to make it in the 1960s. Some fans came down to watch the amateurs play because of the rough way the game was played. Tom Jeffire, kneeling second from left, was one of the coaches and was also the Olympia operations manager. Art Whalen, seen here standing first on the left, was the general manager.

On the right is a program from the professional lacrosse team, the Detroit Olympics, which cost 50¢. The Olympics lost the professional playoff championship to the New Westminster Salmon Bellies of British Columbia, Canada.

Record promoter Tom Schlessinger and Building Superintendent Art Whalen try to put the squeeze on singer Paul Anka at a visit to the Olympia. At one Red Wing game, he dropped the ceremonial opening face-off puck. Anka, a Canadian by birth, did manage to play in a few pickup games with local celebrities.

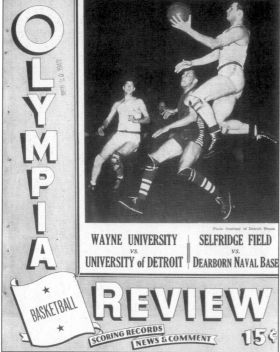

This was a war years basketball program dated February 20, 1943. The four-team tournament featured Wayne University against the University of Detroit, and Selfridge Field vs. Dearborn Naval Base. During the war, many teams of top collegiate caliber sprung up around the country on military bases as players from all over joined or were drafted into the armed services.

Among the many features that appeared at the Olympia Stadium were the famed Lipizzaner show-horses from the Spanish Riding School, located behind the Hapsburgs in Vienna, Austria. The horses are trained for precision riding and drills, plus they are able to jump and kick in mid air. On the right is a ticket from the November 21, 1975 performance. The ticket refers to them as the "World Famous Royal Lipizzan Stallion." The ticket cost was $6.50.

Many of the recording groups made stops to perform at the Olympia Stadium. Singers included Justin Haywood (above) and Harry Chaffin (below).

Another of the popular groups that appeared in Detroit was Emerson, Lake and Palmer (above). James Taylor (below) was still recording into the 21st century.

Lawrence Welk became a household name during the 1960s and '70s, especially with the older generation, with his television show *The Lawrence Welk Show*. Accordion player Myron Florin was one of the most popular performers on the show.

Sheila and Sherry Aldrich join the Otweil Twins in singing for the audience.

Five
HOCKEY AND THE
DETROIT RED WINGS

Seen here are two of the players from the early days of the Falcons and Red Wings franchise: Red Wings defenseman Rollie Roulston (left) and Olympic forward Carson Cooper (right). Cooper joined the Cougars in their second NHL season in 1927. In his third season the name was changed to the Falcons. Carson's last game in the NHL was on March 22, 1932, while playing for the Falcons. Roulston's first game with the Red Wings was on March 22, 1936. He was a member of the 1937 Red Wings Stanley Cup team.

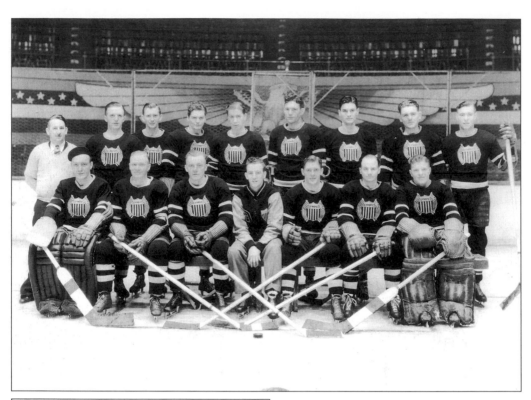

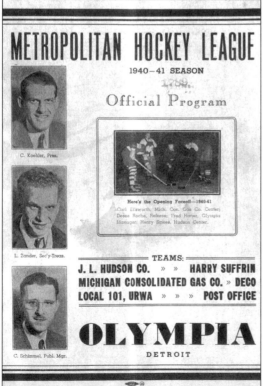

The Detroit Olympics team was a Wings farm club in the 30s. Many of the players moved up and down between the two clubs, one night with the Wings, the next with the Olympics, depending how Jack Adams was feeling that day. They are, from left to right: (standing) Trainer Tommy Anderson, Yank Boyd, Knulker Irvin, Ronnie Moffatt, Rollie Roulston, Norm Walker, Burr Williams, and Mud Bruneteau; (seated) Norm Smith, Ted Graham, Carson Cooper, Manager Donny Hughes, Wally Kilrea, Connie King, and Walter Turk Broda.

This program is from the 1940-41 Metropolitan Hockey League.

Injured players cheer on their teammates in the 1937 playoffs. They are, from left to right: Doug Young, Larry Aurie, and Rollie Roulston. Young was the captain of the club. Roulston broke his leg on January 25, 1937, and missed the rest of the season.

The Wings celebrate after winning the 1937 Stanley Cup with a 3-0 victory over the Rangers on April 15. They are, from left to right: Johnny Sorrell, Herbie Lewis, Hec Kilrea, Mud Bruneteau, Pete Kelly, and Scotty Bowman.

Seen here is the Olympia Stadium in the '30s. Note that parking was allowed along the Grand River. The Olympia sign stuck out so it could be seen for quite a distance when lit up at night. Hooker Street, on the left, still had homes on it. Note that there was a large window in the front

on the building. Later, the whole window area was bricked up and a large Red Wings crest was painted in its place. A new marquee was also added to Olympia Stadium. There were several stores in front, but the only one that survived into the '60s was the drug store on the corner.

This was the championship Olympic team in 1935-36, when Detroit was known as the "City of Champions." The Wings, Tigers, and Lions were all winners in this era, and Joe Louis was the boxing champion of the world. Seen here, from left to right, are: (standing) trainer Art Bordeaux, J Gallagher, Gene Carrigen, Rollie Roulston, Burr Williams, coach Donnie Hughes, Fred Herberts, Johnny Sherf, and trainer Ernie Burton; (seated) Turk Broda, Carl Liscombe, Art Giroux, Ronald Hudson, Wilf Starr, Don Deacon, and Led Tooke.

This is the official 1938-39 team photo. Note that the team carried only one goaltender. One of the young rookies up from the minors was Sid Abel (fourth from the right). Abel was lucky to make this photo, as he was only up for a couple games from the Pittsburgh Hornets. Abel's first NHL game was on November 15, 1938, against the Rangers.

Dapper-smiling Wings defenseman Leo Reise signs for a fan in the 1940s. Hat, suit, tie, and dress coat were required attire at the Olympia Stadium. Woman at games in this era often wore white gloves, and always a hat.

Captain Ted Lindsay gives team owner Marguerite Norris a kiss after winning the 1955 Stanley Cup. On the left is General Manager Jack Adams. Wonder where Jolly Jack got that tie? This was the last time the Wings would win a Cup, until the 1990s.

Celebrating "Jack Adams Night" in Detroit are a few of the Red Wings main-stays during their seven league championships and four Stanley Cups in the early '50s: Marty Pavelich (left), Jack "I'm Jack" Adams (center), and Ted Lindsay (right).

This is the 1953 Red Wings team in civilian clothes. Note the argyle socks on the guys in front. The players, from left to right, are: (first row) Alex Delvecchio, Wally Crossman, Tony Leswick, Fred Glover, Marty Pavelich, and Lefty Wilson; (second row) unknown, Jack Adams, Sid Abel, Tommy Ivan, Fred Hainer, and Leo Riese; (third row) Marcel Pronovost, Vic Stasiuk, Terry Sawchuk, Gordie Howe, Glenn Skov, and Bob Goldham; (fourth row) Red Kelly, Carl Mattson, Metro Prystai, Ted Lindsay, and Benny Woit.

The youngest player to play for the Wings was Harry Lumley, who was signed from the Barrie Colts at age 16. His first two Red Wings games were December 19 and 23, 1943 (during the war years). He was 17 years, 1 month, 8 days old when he played his first game. He lost both games: 6-2 to the Rangers and 7-1 to Chicago. He was inducted into the Hall of Fame in 1980.

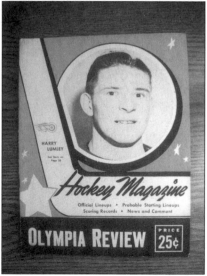

This is a Montreal at Detroit program from the December 22, 1946 game featuring Harry Lumley on the cover. Montreal won that game 4-2.

A few rows behind the visiting team's bench was Mrs. Adams' private box. Her husband Jack had a similar box behind the Red Wings' bench. Between periods, Mrs. Adams would get on the visitors case, as they had to walk next to her to get to their dressing room. One of her favorite targets was the New York Rangers' Goalie Gump Worsley.

Armand "Bep" Guidolin played two seasons with the Wings in the late 40s. He was also the youngest player to play in the NHL, the youngest in the playoffs, and the youngest to score a goal. He was 16 years, 11 months old in 1942, when he played his first game for the Boston Bruins.

During the late '40s the Red Wings were always making personal appearances to publicize their team. Free Autographs were always given out as part of being a professional athlete. Shown above signing for young fans are Gordie Howe, Red Kelly, Black Jack Stewart, Marty Pavelich, and Harry Lumley.

The Wings get together at Grosse Isle Country Club for their annual party in the '50s. The team members, from left to right, are: Metro Prystai, Marcel Pronovost, Red Kelly, Lefty Wilson, Bill Dineen, Marty Pavelich, Jim Skinner, Murray Costello, Alex Delvecchio, Jack Higgins, Dutch Reibel, John Buyck, Gordie Howe, Glen Hall, Ted Lindsay, Carl Mattson, and Larry Hillman.

One of the memorable road games the Wings played was on February 2, 1954, at Marquette Prison, in Michigan's Upper Peninsula in the dead of winter. The athletic director at the prison, Oakie Brumm, arranged the game with the Wings flying in. In the afternoon the Wings played outdoors at the prison. In the evening they played the Marquette Sentinels senior team indoors.

The Wings used the Pullar Stadium in Sault St. Marie, Michigan, in the Upper Peninsula, for training camp for several years in the 1950s. The I-75 highway and Mackinac Bridge (opened in 1957) was not opened, so it took the players a long time to reach Detroit after camp, having to take a car ferry across the Straits of Mackinac.

Getting ready for a road trip in the 1950s, the whole gang poses for a photo in front of the bus. Note Red Kelly in the back row with his green derby on. GM Jack Adams is in the front row center.

Enjoying an evening out at the Randall's home is Red Kelly, Marty Pavelich, Vic Stasiuk, Metro Prystai, Bob Randall, and photographer Roy Bash.

Returning from Sunday Mass in Boston in the 1950s, the Wings headed for breakfast and a morning skate before an evening game against the Bruins. Seen here, from left to right, are: Billy Dea, Ted Lindsay, Red Kelly, Marcel Pronovost, Metro Prystai, Warren Godfrey, Marty Pavelich, and Norm Ullman. As usual, all the players were dressed in ties, suits, and topcoats.

The Red Wings enjoyed dinner at Ma Shaw's boarding house in Detroit. Many of the Wings were bachelors and cooking wasn't high on the list of players' skills—thus many roomed together. Dinner at Ma Shaw's that night was spaghetti, and Ma Shaw is helped by Marty Pavelich to serve his teammates. From left to right, they are: Gordie Howe, Lefty Wilson, Metro Prystai, Ted Lindsay, Ma Shaw, Pavelich, Alex Delvecchio, Glenn Skov, and Tony Leswick. The players tended to stick together off the ice, taking in bowling and personal appearances regularly.

At a dinner function sponsored by
Stroh's Brewery in Detroit is where
players and friends enjoyed the meal.
Facing the camera, from left to right,
are: Metro Prystai and his date, Marty
Pavelich, Red Kelly (foreground), and
Ma Shaw. Seated behind with a
band-aid on his ear is goalie Terry
Sawchuk, beside Lefty Wilson.

The Wings were always happy to lend
their names to charities. Here Marty
Pavelich and Captain Red Kelly
(1956–58) pose with a poster child
prior to a Red Wings game.

The Wings return to Detroit after the famous St. Patrick's Day riots of March 17, 1955. Arriving at Michigan Central Station in Detroit, from left to right, are Bill Dineen, unknown, Jim "Red Eye" Hay, Jack Adams, Marty Pavelich, Dutch Reibel, Red Kelly, and Alex Delvecchio.

Seen here waiting for a cab, from left to right, are: Bill Dineen, Marcel Bonin, Marty Pavelich, and Red Kelly. Jack Higgins is in the background with his bag.

Leaving the station, from left to right, are:
Jack Adams, Red Kelly, Bill Dineen,
Marty Pavelich, and Alex Delvecchio—as
the police motorcycle halts traffic.

Gordie Howe carries son Marty as they
leave the station. Prior to the game the
night before in Montreal, NHL President
Clarence Campbell had suspended
Montreal's Rocket Richard for the rest of
the season and the playoffs for hitting an
official. The game Saturday night at the
Montreal Forum was halted at the end of
the first period with Detroit leading 4-1.
Someone threw a smoke bomb in the
Forum and people started to panic. Outside
a crowd started to break windows and start
a riot. The Detroit press was rushed to the
Wings dressing room and the team was
hurried out with a police escort. Then they
had to wait two hours in the train station
for the train, as the streets of Montreal
were experiencing the famous Rocket
Richard-St. Patrick's Day Riot.

STAR CUTTER CITY CHAMPIONS 58-59

The amateur hockey program in Detroit really started to grow in the 1950s. The Olympia Stadium was good about loaning out their ice to help local teams. In the '50s, the only indoor ice rinks were at the State Fair, Ice Flair on the east side, University of Michigan in Ann Arbor, and Windsor Arena. In the late '50s and early '60s, local communities started to build their own indoor facilities. One of the best-known local teams in the late '50s was the Star Cutter team, who were the city champions in 1958-59. Seen here, the team poses in front of the display case across from the Red Wings dressing room. At one time, the Stanley Cup and other NHL trophies were on display here all year long. Yet, during the playoffs, a couple of Canadiens' fans tried to take the Stanley Cup out of the display during a game, but were quickly caught by the police.

The team lineup, from left to right, is: (front row) Butch Cox, Brad Lawton, Larry Bercel, and Johnny O'Dell; (middle row) Red Belkany, Dickie Devine, Jimmy Smith, Captain Gil Konkle, Joe Zee, and Troy Harper; (back row) Roger Taylor, Ross MacDonald, Wally Rakecky, Coach Art Thomas, Trainer Don Travers, Jim Howlin, and Ron Nozzle.

88

Not all the games ended in favor of the Wings at the Olympia Stadium. On May 6, 1966, Henri Richard scored in overtime on a controversial goal and the Canadiens won the Cup in Detroit on Olympia ice. In the photo accepting the Cup, from left to right, are: Claude Provost, Jim Roberts, Gump Worsley, Gilles Tremblay, Captain Jean Beliveau, and Yvan Cournoyer.

President Clarence Campbell presents the Stanley Cup to the Chicago Black Hawks' Captain Eddie Litzenberger after they won the championship in Detroit in 1961. The players at that time didn't put on big emotional displays and carry the Cup overhead around the ice. Most of the time, the players disbanded and went home for the summer. It wasn't until the '60s, with more TV exposure, that more emotional wins were shown and parades held after the finals.

Lowell MacDonald (left, #8) drinks a pregame cup of coffee as Alex Delvecchio ties his pants and Gordie Howe laces his skates while talking with someone, during pre-game preparations in the Wings dressing room. Ted Hampton, on the right, seems to be psyching himself up for the game. The dressing rooms in the old arenas were quite small and the players just hung their clothes on a hook behind where they sat.

In this early-1960s photo, a Wings coach heads out of the Wings dressing room door toward the ice. The metal door posted the warning, "No Admittance at any time," but this wasn't always enforced before and after games.

Seated on one of the Wings many travel trunks, the 1955 stars chat with new coach, Jim Skinner. Standing is Gordie Howe and Coach Skinner, while Red Kelly and Captain Ted Lindsay are seated from left to right. The Wings went on in Skinner's rookie season to win the league title by two points, and the 1955 Stanley Cup. The Wings beat out Toronto in four straight games, and then beat out the Montreal Canadiens four games to three, as Alex Delvecchio scored two goals in the final game on April 14, 1955. This was to be the last Stanley Cup Detroit would win at Olympia. From 1956 to 1960 Montreal would win five straight Stanley Cups.

When Lippmans Sporting Goods on Michigan and Washington Blvd. closed in 1959, several of the salesmen started their own sporting goods stores. Names like East Side Sports, Blackburns, and Olympic Sporting Goods took over. On June 19, 1959, Olympic Sporting Goods opened on Livernois (also known as the Avenue of Fashion) and Six Mile. At the opening, six of the Wings made a personal appearance. Seen here, from left to right, are: (top row) the Fishman brothers; (standing) Johnny Wilson, Gordie Howe, Warren Godfrey, Left Wilson, Elliott Trumbull, and Sid Abel.

This ad appeared in the November 23, 1965 issue of the *Detroit Free Press*. Note the top seat prices. This was also the year that the Great Lakes Invitational College Hockey Tournament started on December 21-22. The original four teams included Toronto, Colorado, Boston, and Michigan Tech.

Goaltender Dennis Riggins models a new type of goalie mask. It was used for a while before it was soon dismissed because it kept fogging up. Lefty Wilson started then to experiment with different types of custom-made masks, fitted to the players face.

The Wings' doctors and their wives are relaxing at a game. They sat behind the bench, directly in front of Jack Adams' box. They had the end seats so they could go to the players quickly in an emergency. Seated, from left to right, are: Doris Kosley, Genevieve and Dr. Jack Finley, and Dr. Milton Kosley.

During the 1976-77 season, Larry Wilson took over the job as head coach of the Red Wings. His brother John went to become the head coach of the Colorado Rockies. John had coached the Red Wings for 145 games during the 1971–73 seasons, while brother Larry coached for 36 games in the 1976–77 seasons. Neither coached the Wings in the playoffs. John had a 67 wins to 3 wins lead over Larry with the Wings. Both were members of the Wings' 1950 Stanley Cup team. On January 2, 1977, Colorado beat Detroit 6-4, on the 13th Detroit won 4-2 at Colorado, and on the 20th Colorado won 3-2 in Detroit.

Former coach and Assistant General Manager Jim Skinner gets ready to present Vaclav Nedomansky of Hodonin, Czechoslovakia, with awards for the most goals scored (38) and most points (73) for the Wings in the 1978-79 season, along with the Hockey Writers Trophy and the Gormley trophy.

On August 8, 1978, Rogie Vachon signed a contract to play goal for the Detroit Red Wings as a restricted free agent; the Los Angles Kings received Dale McCourt as compensation. As his wife gives him a kiss and a hug, Rogie's agent and General Manager Ted Lindsay look on. Rogie played two years for Detroit, winning 30 games, losing 57 and tying 19. For the two years that Vachon was with Detroit, they failed to make the playoffs.

The Wings delegation board an Air Canada plane for the October 10, 1964 All Star Game in Toronto. The All Stars beat the Leafs 3-2. Before expansion in 1967-68, the Stanley Cup Champions played the All Stars. Seen boarding, from left to right, are: Lefty Wilson, Elliott Trumbull, Johnny Mitchell, Alex Delvecchio, Sid Abel, Gordie Howe, and Norm Ullman

Wings Scout Jack Patterson watches the game from the press box. Patterson was an NHL linesman before joining the Wings as a scout.

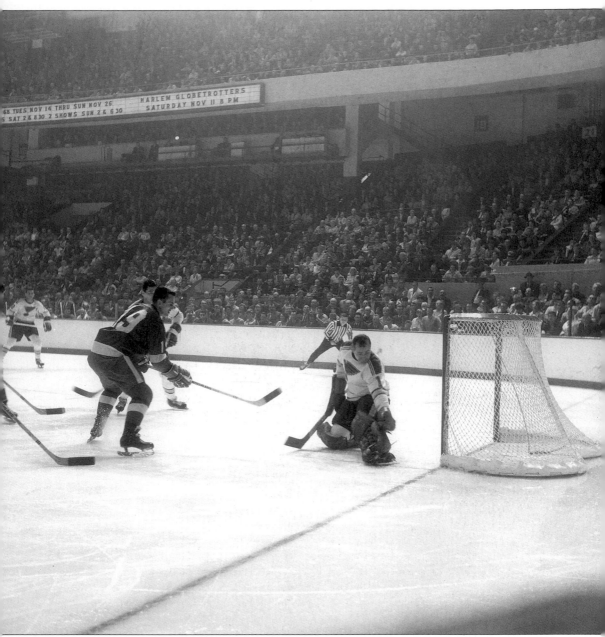

This is the first goal at Olympia scored on an expansion team. Paul Henderson (#19) beats Glen Hall of St. Louis at 15:01 of the third period to give the Wings a 1-0 win. Hall was the Wings and Black Hawks goalie before being drafted by the Blues. Roger Crozier got the shutout for the Wings. Henderson would later score the winning goal for Team Canada against the Russians in 1972, in Russia, as millions of people around the world watched the game on TV.

Baseball or Hockey? That was the question Detroiter Dennis Ribant had to face in 1960. As a youngster growing up in Detroit, Denny played baseball and hockey. He was good enough for the Wings to go after him and send him to their Junior B team in Burlington. The following season he was up in Junior A with Hamilton. In the off-season he was playing in the minors with the Braves, after signing for a $15,000 bonus. That's when he had to make a decision—hockey or baseball? There wasn't any money in hockey and it would have taken him a few years to reach the NHL, so baseball was his choice. He did pitch in Detroit on the Tigers in 1968, but was traded before they won the World Series.

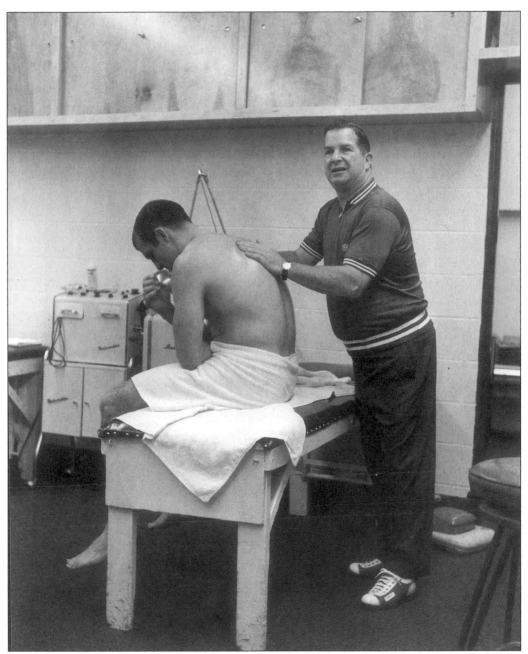

Ross "Lefty" Wilson was "Mr. Everything" for the Red Wings during his tenure as trainer. A native of Toronto, Lefty was a good enough baseball player to join the Boston Braves' farm team. He also played goal for the Omaha Knights. After time for service in World War II, he returned to play baseball and hockey. He spent three seasons with the Indianapolis Capitols before joining the Red Wings as the assistant trainer in 1951. As the assistant trainer, he was also the back-up goalie. If a goaltender got hurt in a game Lefty had to replace him, no matter if it was for the Wings or the visitors. Lefty played in three games for Detroit, Toronto, and Boston during his career, allowing only one goal. Here, Lefty is in his medical room treating defenseman Carl Brewer.

Coach and General Manager Sid Abel congratulates Gordie Howe (#9), who had just broken Maurice "The Rocket" Richard's scoring record of 544 goals. On November 10, 1963, while short handed, Bill Gadsby and Billy McNeil moved the puck up the ice to Gordie Howe who scored on Montreal's Charlie Hodge to become the greatest goal scorer in the history of hockey.

Terry Sawchuk, recorded his 94th shutout as the Wings won 3-0. Standing behind Abel are Pete Maurdias (left) and trainer Danny Olesevich (right). To their right is Larry Jeffrey. Seated on the bench is Andre Pronovost, behind him is Wally Crossman, and the gentleman behind Wally with the glasses is sportswriter Joe Falls.

For 25 years of service as the Wings team dentist, Dr. Florian Muske, with his wife Justine, receive congratulations from Gary Bergman (note the sideburns). Handling the MC's job is Budd Lynch.

Enjoying a night out, from left to right, are: Red Wings Parker MacDonald, Roger Crozier, Floyd Smith (with the eye patch), Gary Gergman, and Dr. Jack Finley.

Gordie Howe holds up puck #544 in
the Wings dressing room for the
photographers. On October 30,
1963, at Olympia, the Canadiens
beat the Wings 6-4 as Howe scored
his goal to tie the Rocket's record.
Seated to the left is Alex
Delvecchio.

New Wings coach Doug Barkley
talks to the media after replacing
Ned Harkness in 1970. In 1971 he
was replaced by Johnny Wilson, but
was rehired in 1974.

Ready to play with his sons, Mark and Marty, against the Red Wings in a charity game, the Howe family is introduced on the ice. Seen from left to right are: Gordie, Cathy, Colleen, Murray, Mark, and Marty.

Joining his sons' junior team, Howe watches the action with coach Ernie Asadoorian.

The championship Olympia Agency Junior team poses for a group photo in the Olympia Room. Seated third from the left is Bobby Goodenow, who went on to a collegiate hockey career, a law degree, and is now head of the National Hockey League Players Association.

After the Junior Wings disbanded in the 1960s, the Olympia had a recreational junior league representing different areas of the city. Representing the west side was the Adray Appliance team, led by Larry Kosiba.

The Junior Wings pose with their championship trophy. In the back is coach Jimmy Peters, and on the right is General Manager Dan Distell.

Seen here during training camp at Olympia is the Red Wings training staff, from left to right: Lefty Wilson, Gerry Strong (Fort Worth Wings), and Danny Olesevich.

Enjoying a win after a game, from left to right, are: Gordie Howe, Johnny Wilson, Norm Ullman, Marcek Pronovost, and Terry Sawchuk.

Checking out the action at a dinner party, from left to right, are: Dean Prentice, Floyd Smith (with the eye patch), Dr. Finley, and Ted Lindsay. The party was held at the Grosse Isle Country Club.

Coach Pete Daniels poses with his Red Wings Alumni team. This club preceded the Junior Wings at the Olympia Stadium. Pete was also an off-ice official at Olympia for the National Hockey League.

Coach Pete Daniels talks to his young hopefuls during training camp. From left to right, are: Tom Petrie, Mike Grey, Mike D'Agostino, Mike Barrie, Chet Karwowski, Harold Herman, Jerry Serediuk, and Ray Demers.

Behind the stands *Hockey Night* in Canada had set up a booth to cover the Toronto-Detroit playoffs. Here Ward Cornell interviews Jerry Toppazzini and Harry Howell.

The Howe family actually had four members playing in the NHL. Gordie's brother, Vic, who was one year younger, played for the New York Rangers in the 1950s. He played parts of three seasons in New York.

This youngster in a 1967 photo, a member of the 1968 and '69 Montreal Stanley Cup teams, was traded to Detroit in 1971, along with Bill Collins and Guy Charron for Frank Mahovlich. He went on to set scoring records for the Wings, netting 52 goals in the 1972-73 season, and 51 goals in 1973-74. He also led the team in scoring in 1972-73. Noted for his blazing shot from the face-off circle, he is now the TV color analyst for the Red Wings. Recognize him? Try Mickey Redmond.

The Norris family, besides owning the Olympia, also had interest in the Bruins and Black Hawks. This is the famous Chicago Stadium with fans lined up for tickets. At one time people said the NHL stood for the Norris House League.

These two gentlemen were assigned to help the visiting team trainers. Al Parent and Len Fletcher would sometimes arrive at 4 a.m. to help the trainers unload, and then return in the afternoon to get ready for the game. Fletcher was also the Alumni's trainer.

1953 Red Wings

BEST winning habit in Detroit sports belongs to the Red Wings. It has made them the only National Hockey League team to take five straight regular season titles. (Colorphotos by James Kilpatrick.)

Top Row: Left to right: Benny Woit, Marcel Pronovost, Bob Goldham. Second Row: Glen Skov, Alex Delvecchio, Ted Lindsay, Marty Pavelich, Metro Prystai. Third Row: Terry Sawchuk, Coach Tommy Ivan, Manager Jack Adams (circle), Gordon Howe. Fourth Row: Reg Sinclair, Johnny Wilson, Marcel Bonin. Bottom Row: Trainer Carl Mattson, Asst. Trainer Lefty Wilson, Leon (Red) Kelly, Tony Leswick, Jim (Red Eye) Hay.

This was a page from the *Detroit News* featuring the 1953 edition of the Wings. Coming off the 1952 Stanley Cup Championship in a record eight games, the 1953 team went out in the first round of the playoffs, loosing to the Boston Bruins four games to two. Needless to say, Jack Adams was on the phone arranging trades for the 1954 season.

112

Six

FINAL MEMORIES

The women behind the main counter by Grand River get ready to serve the customers during the final season at the Olympia Stadium. Many of the employees never went on to the new Joe Louis Arena in December of 1979. The crew on duty, from left to right, are: Elsie Dargan, unknown, Mary Bottrell, and Lydia Arnatt.

When the new addition and escalator was installed in the summer of 1974, the Wings went on the offense to sell seats high in the balcony. The new escalator helped as climbing 101 steps was a little taxing on older fans. The new press box was also moved to the balcony and the old one

WE'RE EXCITED ABOUT NEXT SEASON

The Red Wings, under Alex Delvecchio, have a new look. The youth movement, started last season, carries into the 1974-75 campaign . . .

- a new divisional alignment and playoff format
- two new NHL teams
- an attractive 41 game home schedule
- Hockey's greatest stars play at Olympia. NHL greats like Bobby Orr, Stan Mikita, Brad Park, Bobby Clarke and Yvan Cournoyer will be here to play the Red Wings led by Mickey Redmond, Marcel Dionne, Jimmy Rutherford, Nick Libett and Bryan Watson.
- BE PART OF THE 1974-75 RED WING SEASON.
- RESERVE YOUR SEATS NOW — CALL 895-7000.

YOU'LL GET A CHARGE OUT OF OLYMPIA!!

- A totally new concept in ticket service!!
- Now Olympia Stadium and Bank of the Commonwealth make it possible for you to purchase tickets to any event at Olympia on your Master Charge.
- For the first time ever, simply order by mail, telephone, or at the Olympia Box Office. Give your Master Charge Card Number and purchase tickets to Red Wing games, ice shows, roller games, wrestling and all other Olympia attractions.
- Buy your season tickets this way too.
- It's convenience personified.
- B.C.ing you with Master Charge at Olympia.

TRY IT — YOU'LL LIKE IT!

Call 895-7000 to arrange for Olympia Box Office personnel to show you the seats available for the 1974-75 Red Wing season.

DETROIT RED WINGS
SEASON TICKET PLAN

	Season Tickets Per Ticket	Individual Games Per Ticket
Arena Boxes	$410	$10
Exec. Lounge	$410	$10
Arena, Lower	$328	$8
Wing Hi Boxes	$287	$7
Promenade	$287	$7
Arena, Upper	$246	$6
Mezzanine	$205	$5

PLEASE NOTE: NO INCREASE IN TICKET PRICES

was converted to luxury seating. This was the brochure that was sent to all season ticket holders and businesses.

Budd Lynch and Captain Dennis Hextall made the trophy presentations at the start of the 1978 season. Hextall was the son of Rangers' Hall of Famer Bryan Hextall and brother of Bryan Jr. who also played for the Wings. During Hextall's first two seasons with the Wings, they didn't make the playoffs, but in 1978 they did, finishing second to Montreal. They took out Atlanta two games to zip, before losing to the Canadiens four games to one.

During the final season (fall of 1979), the Wings and NHL announced that the 1980 All-Star Game would be played at the new Joe Louis Arena. Making the announcement in the Olympia Room are NHL President John Ziegler, owner Bruce Norris, General Manager Ted Lindsay, and Wings Vice President Lincoln Cavalieri.

This is a pair of tickets from the college hockey events held at the Olympia. The Great Lakes Tournament was started back in the winter of 1965. Today they are a major attraction at the Joe Louis Arena.

This is the Stanley Cup brawl in Detroit on April 6, 1951. Ted Lindsay lies on the ice after being smashed into the boards. Montreal's Bernie Geoffrion yells at Bob Goldham, putting a headlock on an unidentified Canadien while Red Kelly (right) moves in on the action. During the 1950s, the Montreal–Red Wings games were the most fiercely contested events in the NHL. Note the screen on top of the boards and the fans. Most of the men and women wore hats to the games in that era.

Gordie Howe was more than just a
hockey player. He often worked out
with the Detroit Tigers and his friend
Al Kaline. Here, he smacks a shot in
the batting cage.

Bill Clements was quite an amateur
hockey player and official locally. He
officiated in the local recreation and
college leagues before joining the
NHL as a linesman. Later, he became
head of the off-ice NHL officials at the
Olympia.

Back in the 1966-67, a youngster with the Boston Bruins was changing the way the defense played the game. As an 18 year old, Bobby Orr was a terrific skater and puck handler—with a great shot. Orr thrilled fans with his end-to-end rushes with great speed. He was the rookie of the year in 1967 and in his second season was voted the best defenseman in the NHL. His knees didn't last and after only ten seasons with Boston he was forced to retire. He did try to play for the Hawks afterwards, but his knees would not let him, and he retired for good six games into the 1978 season.

In the old days, in 1927 to be exact, a young man came to work at the Olympia Stadium. He did almost every job in the building well into the 1960s. He was an usher and at one time used to be on the ice detail. That man, William Opalewski, is shown here shoveling the ice between periods during a game. For hockey games and ice shows the ice was done by hand. Mr. Opalewski had his sons and other family members working at the Olympia. It was sort of ironic that he died on the job at Olympia, and his son Bernie died on the job at the Joe Louis Arena.

The greatest hockey player to ever wear a Red Wings jersey was Gordie Howe. Old #9 (he originally wore #17) is seen here receiving the Hart Trophy, for the sixth time, a record in the Original 6. Presenting the trophy is President Clarence Campbell, as owner Bruce Norris watches.

From the 1930s until the building closed in 1980, these two former goaltenders were fixtures at the Olympia Stadium. Lefty Wilson (left) joined the Wings in 1951 as an assistant trainer and back-up goaltender. Normie Smith came up in the 1930s with the Detroit Olympics, and graduated to the Red Wings in 1934. He was acquired from the St. Louis Eagles of the NHL in 1934 and retired in 1938 after winning two Stanley Cups. During World War II, he made a comeback, when the war affected the lineups of many of its teams.

Two of the mainstays for almost a half-century at the Olympia were Mrs. Helen Adams, wife of longtime General Manager Jack Adams and owner Bruce Norris. Norris sold the team to Mike Ilitch in 1982.

Toward the end of its days, graffiti was appearing on the building and most of the windows were plastered up. Today one question still puzzles me. Who was Bootsy Rubberband?

Some of the Olympia concession workers who went over to work at the new Joe Louis Arena included, from left to right: (back row) Faylin Whitefoot, Teresa Betterly, Helen Vick, Eleanor Buchanan. Sitting May Ogle, Mary Fuller, and Diana Warchol; (front, on floor) Anna O'Grady and Lydia Arnatt.

During the 1967 Riots in Detroit, much of the area around the stadium was looted or burned. On the next block, the Olympia Stop N' Shop was totally stripped to the bare walls and destroyed. This had been the original drug store on the corner of the Olympia. The owners did reopen at the Broadway Market downtown.

The back part of the Olympia was torn out first to emit light into the building. Many fans went into the building and took souvenirs and chairs before the building was finally down in 1986.

The claws start to tear down the Olympia Stadium. The first area to go was the Red Wings dressing room. Cuyahoga Wrecking of Cleveland was the winning bidder to tear the building down.

This is the Grand River end of the building. The scoreboard has been stripped and seats have been carried out. On Saturdays and Sundays, crews of collectors would come down to salvage seats. Six years of rain leakage and no heat in the building soiled most of them.

This is the Olympia Crew at the new Joe Louis Arena. Waiting to check in for the evening, these former Olympia employees relax on seats brought over from the Olympia Stadium. They are: Nancy McCracken (kneeling), Eleanor Bucanan, Mary Ogle, Mary Fuller, Bridgett Kellums, Teresa Betterly, and Diana Warchol. On floor are Faylin Whitefoot and Lydia Arnatt.

The final photo of the guys by the cornerstone. No one even knew the existence of the corner stone, which was on the McGraw and Grand River end of the Olympia. Several people tried to take it off the building but only succeeded in ruining it.

Standing on McGraw looking toward Grand River are Jim Omilian, Robert "Red" Wimmer, Gerry Szweda, Greg Innis, Mike DesRosiers, and Dwayne LaBakas. One fan wrote in chalk on the side of the building its epitaph: "Thanks for the Memories."

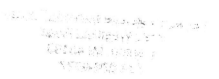